Crafting the Perfect

Wedding

From Saying "Yes" to
The Big Day and Beyond

ANITA LOUISE CRANE

WATSON-GUPTILL PUBLICATIONS / NEW YORK

First published in 2004 by Watson-Guptill Publications, a division of VNU Business Media, Inc., 770 Broadway, New York, NY 10003 www.watsonguptill.com

ISBN: 0-8230-0994-7
Library of Congress Cataloging-in-Publication Data is available from the Library of Congress.

Senior Acquisitions Editor: Joy Aquilino
Editor: Elizabeth Wright
Designer: Barbara Balch
Production Manager: Hector Campbell

Printed in Malaysia
First printing, 2004
1 2 3 4 5 6 7 8 9 / 08 07 06 05 04

Special thank-you's go to: Chris and Shannon Duh
for the use of their wedding invitation;
Faye and David; and Deborah Warren.

This book is dedicated to

Jeremy and Leslie.

Contents

Introduction

For most people, the dream of a perfect wedding begins long before they become engaged. Once you've accomplished the hard part—actually finding the person you want to spend the rest of your life with—planning a wedding should seem easy in comparison. Trying to make the most important day in your life live up to your dreams can be far from easy, however. That's why I've written this book. *Crafting the Perfect Wedding* will help you create a day full of perfect moments and simple, elegant, affordable details no one will forget.

Crafting the Perfect Wedding will guide you chronologically through all the events you'll need to plan, with charming ideas for everything from handmade party invitations to wedding dress and hair accessories to table decorations, and you do not have to be an advanced seamstress or crafter to make them. Each project's level of difficulty is rated on a scale of one to three (see "Levels of Difficulty" on p. 9). Please note that the sewing projects require *at least* a basic knowledge of stitches and sewing techniques, but most of the other projects can be undertaken by anyone with a beginning to intermediate level of crafting experience. Each has beautiful, inspirational photographs, easy-to-follow step-by-step instructions, and an estimate of how much time and money it will require to complete. *Crafting the Perfect Wedding* is your one-stop reference for all the ideas you'll need to make your dream day a reality. Congratulations and happy crafting!

LEVELS OF DIFFICULTY

Each of the projects in this book has been rated according to the levels of difficulty that are described below.

Level 1: Very easy. Appropriate for a beginning sewer or novice crafter.
Level 2: Moderately easy. An intermediate knowledge of sewing or crafting techniques is required.
Level 3: Fairly difficult. More advanced knowledge of sewing and crafting techniques is required.

STITCH GLOSSARY

This book does not contain instructions for basic hand and machine stitching or sewing techniques. Such guides are widely available at most fabric stores, and many sewing machine manuals contain instructions for basic stitches. The sewing projects in this book assume at least a basic understanding of machine and hand stitching, but definitions of some common terms have been provided here for clarity.

Basting stitch (also called a "running" or "gathering" stitch)
Basting is a temporary stitch most often used in the preparatory phase of sewing. A basting stitch is also used to tuck or sew seams, or to gather fabric to obtain fullness (then referred to in this book as a running or gathering stitch). Thread a needle and knot the end, and insert the needle into the fabric. Make many short, forward stitches, evenly weaving the needle in and out of the fabric before you pull the thread through.

Whipstitch (for joining two edges of material)
The whipstitch holds two edges of material together with tiny, straight, even stitches. It is primarily used to join lace edging, to attach ribbon to the edge of fabric, or to close pillow-cover openings. For this stitch, you insert the needle at a right angle from the back edge through to the front edge, picking up only one or two threads at a time.

Joining seams on a sewing machine
When joining seams (as you would when making the satin and tulle bow on p. 94, for example), pin the edges of your fabric together, right-sides facing, with the pins at right angles to the seamline and their heads toward the seam allowance. This way your seams will be held in place accurately, and in a position in which they can be stitched over by most sewing machines. Instead of pinning, you can also baste the seamline in place before stitching on the machine, and then remove the basting after you have finished machine stitching.

Grading and notching curved seams
When seam allowances are turned together in one direction, they must be graded and notched (as they are in our round ring pillow on p. 102). Sew around, leaving an opening for turning the fabric right-side-out when you are finished stitching the edges. Cut one edge of the stitched seam allowance so that it's *graded* ¼ inch shorter than the other edge. Now, at ½- inch to 1-inch intervals, cut a *v*-shaped notch all around. Be careful not to cut the seam-stitching. Turn the fabric right-side-out and iron it lightly. Your seam should lie flat without puckering.

Saying "Yes!"

Congratulations—you've decided to get engaged! You will be dying to tell everyone, but whom do you tell first? Having an engagement party is an excellent way to gather the most important people in your life in one room and formally announce your good news with a toast. Such a gathering allows people to share your happiness in an intimate setting and be part of the first of many chapters in your wedding story.

This is a time of beginnings—a time to not only bask in the glow of a new life, but also begin thinking about what kind of wedding you want. Enjoy the moment, but get those creative wheels rolling, too! This chapter will give you ideas for making your engagement party special and will guide you through the first steps of making your fantasy wedding a reality. The fun projects in this chapter will set the stage for all the romance and drama to come.

We're Engaged!
TO DO LIST

*O*nce you're engaged, simply knowing what you need to do when will make things much more manageable. You don't have to become "bridezilla"—the planning can become part of the fun! The following to do list covers the big things you should take care of right after getting engaged: This list addresses the important details that will ensure that your wedding day is everything you imagined it would be. Tailor the list to suit the style of your wedding and your budget.

ESSENTIALS

❑ Plan the size and type of wedding you want, and set a budget.

❑ Set a date.

❑ If it's within your budget, hire a wedding consultant or buy wedding-planning computer software.

❑ Decide upon and reserve the ceremony and reception sites.

❑ Compile a list of guests, complete with addresses, so you can send announcements and invitations.

❑ Select and purchase wedding rings.

❑ Choose and order your wedding gown. It will take at least three months for a gown to be made.

❑ Plan your honeymoon and make appropriate reservations.

CEREMONY

❑ Reserve the officiant you have chosen.

❑ Choose your bridal attendants and groomsmen.

❑ Choose and book a photographer.

❑ Meet with a florist to discuss the kind and quantity of arrangements you want, and to reserve his or her time.

❑ Order stationery for invitations and thank-you notes.

❑ Send out "save the date" notices (see page 37) with your engagement announcement.

WEDDING PARTY

❑ Choose and order groom's and groomsmen attire.

❑ Choose and order attendants' gowns.

RECEPTION

❑ Decide upon a menu for the reception with the site personnel or a caterer.

❑ Order the wedding cake.

❑ If you're having an at-home or garden reception, reserve any rental equipment you may need, such as tables, chairs, or tents.

❑ Decide on the kind of music you want for the reception and make arrangements for a band or DJ.

Engagement Party Invitations

You can make this charmingly unique engagement party invitation with a simple list of supplies and materials. Invite a group of friends to help. Each person can decorate her card a little differently and truly give these handmade invitations a sense of personality. You can customize these cards further by choosing different colors of cardstock, ribbon, and lace. Save one for the first page of your wedding album.

COST: *About $2 per card* TIME: *30 minutes* LEVEL: *1* WHEN: *6 weeks before the event*

YOU WILL NEED (FOR EACH CARD):

- *Dress form pattern*
- *Tracing paper*
- *Pencil*
- *Plain cards and envelopes*
- *Cardstock in cream or white*
- *Lace edging: 3 inches*
- *Scotch tape: both double-sided and regular*
- *¼-inch-wide organza or lacy ribbon: 10 inches*
- *2-inch-wide wired edge ribbon: 11 inches*
- *A pinch of poly stuffing (optional)*
- *Assorted scraps of lace: 8 inches per card*
- *String pearls for "necklace" (optional): ½ inch*

- *A ballpoint or calligraphy pen*
- *Scissors*
- *Craft glue*

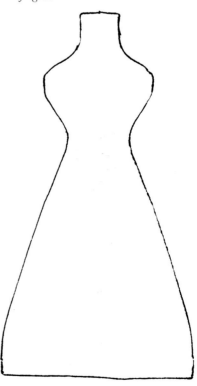

STEP 1. Using tracing paper and pencil, trace the dress-form pattern; use the tracing as a template to cut out the dress form from each piece of cardstock. Attach lace edging to the bottom of the dress with double-sided tape.

STEP 2. Wrap about 4 inches of the organza or lacy ribbon around the bottom of the

dress form just above the lace edging. Tape the ribbon at the back with single-sided scotch tape. Repeat until you have covered the cut out up to the waist. (The tape is on the back of the dress form, so it will not be visible.)

STEP 3. Cut a 3-inch length of wired ribbon for the bodice of the dress. Fold the wired edge down about ⅛ inch and then tuck a tiny pinch of poly stuffing under the fold. Strap the ribbon around the bodice and tape it securely to the back. Tie a length of lace ribbon or one of the scraps of lace around the waist of the dress in a pretty bow and

trim off the excess. Attach string pearls to the neckline of the dress using craft glue. Dot the back of the dress with craft glue and, making sure it is centered, adhere it to the front of the card.

STEP 4. If you have nice handwriting, write your message inside the card with a calligraphy pen or a ballpoint pen. You can also type your message on a computer using an elegant font and print it on a piece of high-quality stationery. Carefully measure and cut the paper to a height and width that will make it perfectly centered when placed inside the card, then precisely paste it there with craft glue.

Beaded Ring Box

A unique, handmade beaded box is a romantic way to present a ring to the bride-to-be or a beautiful place to keep wedding bands until the ceremony. You can make these glittering boxes fairly quickly without spending a lot. Take an ordinary ring or jewelry box and cover it with silver beads or pearls, both of which are available at most craft centers packaged in small plastic bags or plastic tubes containing a hundred or more beads.

❧COST: *About $2 per box* ❧TIME: *Less than 30 minutes* ❧LEVEL: *1* ❧WHEN: *Anytime before the engagement party*

YOU WILL NEED

- *One package or tube (containing at least 100) 30 gram, 3mm silver "Rocailles" beads or, if you want to make a pearl box, two packages (each containing at least 100) of 60 gram, 3mm pearls and one large rhinestone or pearl button.*
- *Ring box (cardboard)*
- *Small craft brush*
- *White tacky glue*
- *Dish for beads*
- *Small cloth*
- *Tweezers (optional)*
- *Pins*

Pour the beads into the dish. Set out the brush, glue, and tweezers. Have a damp cloth available for cleanup. Apply the glue with the brush to one side of the box at a time. Press the glue-side into the dish of beads, rolling back and forth and tapping the beads in place with your fingertips. If necessary, you can use the tweezers to fill in any gaps. Wait until the beads are dry and set before continuing on to the other sides of box. Repeat this step until the box is completely covered with beads. If you want to decorate the lid of the box with a rhinestone or pearl button, glue that on first, and once it's dry, fill the rest of the lid with beads as you did for the other sides of the box. The tacky glue will set quite quickly.

Engagement Party Centerpieces

hether your engagement party is formal or casual, a colorful bouquet of flowers in a unique vase or bowl will give the setting instant grace. The kind of container in which you display the flowers can be as important to the presentation as the kind of blooms you choose, but don't run out and spend a lot of money on a vase! Look through your kitchen for glass jars with attractive shapes and silver teapots and bowls.

We will show you how glass jars with ruffled tulle and ribbon catch the light and give flower arrangements a casual, fresh look. Silver bowls or "biscuit jars" can become elegant centerpieces that reflect the colors of the flowers and your table linen. Make your engagement party sparkle with light and warmth.

Bouquets in Silver

❧ COST: *About $20*
❧ TIME: *5–10 minutes per centerpiece*
❧ LEVEL: *1*
❧ WHEN: *Day before the party*

YOU WILL NEED (FOR ONE SMALL CENTERPIECE):

- *Small to medium silver "container"*
- *½ dozen roses or flowers of your choice*
- *Wet floral foam*
- *Plastic freezer-storage bag, big enough to line your container*
- *Flower cutters or scissors*
- *Water*

Line your container with a plastic bag—this will prevent leakage and possible water damage to your silver. Cut a chunk of floral foam to fit inside the container (it must also fit in the plastic). Soak it in water until it is completely saturated. This usually takes a couple of minutes. Insert the wet floral foam inside the plastic bag. Now cut the flower stems so that they are all about the same length, and arrange them by pushing the stems into the foam. The wet foam will keep the flowers fresh and in place.

Tulle-Wrapped Jars

Nicely shaped jars make wonderful centerpieces, especially for a casual or garden party. The finishing touch of the tulle lends an airy sophistication to the whole arrangement. First you will need to wash the jars and soak them in hot water if they have labels that need to be removed. Use glue remover ("Goo Gone" works well) to remove any stubborn glue. You are by no means limited to the ideas offered here—dress up the jars in any other way your fancy strikes. For example, you could clip crystal beaded garlands to the appropriate size and wrap them around the jar container.

COST: *About $15 per centerpiece* • TIME: *30 minutes* • LEVEL: *1* • WHEN: *1 day before the party*

YOU WILL NEED
(FOR 12 SMALL OR 6 LARGE CENTERPIECES):

- *12 jars*
- *Goo Gone or other glue remover*
- *Tape measure*
- *Approximately 3 yards of tulle netting (for 12 small containers—use 4 yards for 6 large containers)*
- *Ribbon (approximately 12 yards for 12 small containers—18 yards for 6 large containers)*

- *Rubber bands (large and small sizes)*
- *Water*
- *Flowers (amount needed to fill your individual containers)*
- *Beaded garland (optional)*

STEP 1. Remove any labels or glue from the jars by soaking them in hot water and using glue remover. After all the glue is gone, wash and dry the jars thoroughly.

STEP 2. Measure the tulle squares. You will have to custom measure the tulle for each jar, since they will probably all be different sizes. First, measure the jar according to the following guidelines: measure half the width of the bottom of the jar, add that number to the height of the container, add four inches to accommodate the ruffle, and then multiply by two. That will give you the dimensions for the square of tulle you need to cut. Example: 3" width of bottom + 5" height + 4" for ruffle = 12" x 2 = 24" square.

STEP 3. Cut three square layers of tulle according to the measurement you have calculated. Fold the squares in half once, and again. You will then have a smaller square. Trim the raw edges on two sides to turn the square into a circle. The circle does not need to be perfectly round because when you fluff the tulle, the irregular shape of each layer will just add to its airiness.

STEP 4. Set the jar on the center of the tulle layers, gather the tulle up around the neck of the jar (you might need an extra pair of hands for this), and slip a rubber band over the jar neck. Pull, separate, and arrange the tulle. Tie a ribbon around the neck of the jar. Fill the jar with water and flowers.

MORE IDEAS

1. Use the three layers of tulle in different colors for a vibrant effect.

2. Do groupings of three to five small jars on each table, each one holding a different type of flower. Note: Always use odd numbers for your arrangements.

3. Look for seasonal blossoms, leafy branches, and twigs in your backyard that can be used as attractive filler for your flower arrangements.

CHAPTER 2

Planning Your Wedding

wedding is a ceremony uniting a couple, but it is also a joyous occasion that brings circles of friends and family together in celebration. Ideally, a couple should have one year from the date upon which they announce their engagement to plan the actual wedding. Many wedding sites are booked well in advance, and you will want plenty of time to work out all the details involved in such a complex, important event. Most couples want their ceremony to be meaningful and personal, and they want the reception to be fun, festive, and unforgettable. Trying to actually pull that off without becoming stressed out and overwhelmed, however, can be a challenge.

If you have less than six months to plan your wedding, get started as soon as possible. Setting up a schedule with progessive deadlines is the best way to proceed. Be prepared to be flexible, make compromises, and remain receptive to all possibilities. The most important part of a wedding is the joy of the occasion—it is a party!

Where to Start

Give yourself a quiet, pleasant place to focus by cy creating a work space that you use only for matters related to the wedding. Find a corner in your bedroom or elsewhere in your home where you can set up a wedding planning desk. When you sit and work there, everything you need will be in front of you, and you won't have any distractions or interruptions. Here is a list of things you should have on hand that will help you stay on track and on top of things:

- Computer (with wedding-planning software and e-mail and Internet access)
- Phone
- Fax machine if possible
- Bulletin board
- Address book
- Telephone book
- Wedding planning binder
- Reference materials
- CD or tape player
- CD's of possible music for the reception
- Stationery
- Stamps
- Envelopes
- Inspirational photographs or pages from magazines

BRAINSTORMING. Once your space is set up, you can begin making decisions about what kind of wedding you want. Become informed about all the options available to you. At this point, you can cater your dream to the resources available to you and start getting creative! Go through bridal magazines and cut out pictures you like. Organize the pictures by subject and dominant color scheme and think about what made you select those pictures. What elements within them are attractive to you? What decorative details inspire you? Look at dresses, tuxes, table settings, flower arrangements, styles of receptions, colors, and seasonal decorations. Narrow the pictures down to those that most closely match your sense of the kind of wedding you want. Put them in your scrapbook or pin them up on your bulletin board.

CHOOSING YOUR COLOR. Having trouble visualizing a color scheme? Go to the paint store and collect paint color swatches. Group them by hues. Pin them to your bulletin board. Stand back and look at them. You will soon find groupings of colors and hues that complement one another and that you are more drawn to than others. Put different swatches side by side to see how well they work together. Experiment— spread them out on your desk and play. Before you know it, you will find the color scheme that suits your wedding perfectly.

FINDING YOUR MUSIC. When selecting music for your ceremony and reception, play a variety of styles while you are sitting and working. If you are hiring a band for your wedding, get tapes from potential candidates. If you are hiring a DJ for the reception, buy and play a mix of music you like and pick particular songs or artists that would be appropriate and fun.

Making Punch Lists
AND CHECKING THEM TWICE

he four to six months before the wedding is a crucial period. All the arrangements you looked into and reserved right after your engagment should now be booked and confirmed. The big things have been settled; however, don't forget about the little things such as arranging for adequate parking at the ceremony and reception sites, having a plan for inclement weather, arranging for transportation for the wedding party to and from the ceremony and reception, and confirming your reservations for your honeymoon. The following punchlists cover the details—minor and major—that you should take care of a few months before the wedding.

ESSENTIALS

- ❑ Confirm ceremony and reception sites.
- ❑ Confirm order for wedding gown.
- ❑ Confirm reservation for officiant.
- ❑ Confirm booking with wedding photographer.
- ❑ Address and mail wedding invitations.
- ❑ Inform wedding guests where you've chosen to register for gifts.
- ❑ Check on status and delivery date for wedding rings.
- ❑ Meet with photographer to compile a list of important pictures you desire.
- ❑ Apply for wedding license.

CEREMONY

- ❑ Meet with officiant to go over details of ceremony and confirm date.
- ❑ Review and confirm plans for wedding rehearsal and rehearsal dinner.
- ❑ Visit ceremony site to evaluate issues such as parking space, air conditioning, restroom facilities, etc.

- ❏ Discuss receiving line and draw up chart for placement of parents, attendants, and other family members in line. Arrange to have chairs available for older family members.

- ❏ Make any necessary arrangements to accommodate divorced parents in the receiving line and seating for ceremony.

- ❏ Assign someone the task of transferring flower arrangements from the ceremony to the reception site.

WEDDING PARTY

- ❏ Reserve transportation for wedding party to and from ceremony site and reception.

- ❏ Make sure groomsmen have been measured for rental tuxedos or that arrangements are confirmed for other clothing.

- ❏ Arrange final fittings for attendants' gowns.

- ❏ Make gifts for wedding party.

RECEPTION

- ❏ Confirm services of wedding florist and order flowers.

- ❏ Confirm order of wedding cake.

- ❏ Confirm reception date with caterer; go over menu and give caterer the final guest count.

- ❏ Confirm reservation for rental of tables, chairs, tents for outdoor or garden wedding.

- ❏ Review alternate plans for inclement weather if reception will be outdoors.

- ❏ Book music.

- ❏ Make favors for guests.

- ❏ Arrange to have entertainment for any children who will be present.

- ❏ Assign someone the task of helping the photographer identify family members and assembling family and the wedding party for portraits.

- ❏ Make and confirm plans for a place to spend your wedding night.

HONEYMOON

- ❏ Arrange to have someone housesit for you while you are away.

- ❏ Confirm all hotel and travel reservations.

- ❏ Get travelers' checks.

- ❏ Get passports.

- ❏ Arrange for transportation to the airport.

Creating a Storyboard

storyboard is a bulletin board upon which you can lay out the chronology of your wedding visually—from engagement to honeymoon. Pin notes, pictures, and lists for each stage of the wedding, and when you sit at your desk, you can look up and have an immediate sequence of events to orient you. It will help you visualize the look you want for your wedding as well as to spell out your plans and choices. (The board we're showing you here is bare bones so that you can see the fabric backing.) You can frame the bulletin board after you have covered it with fabric or leave it just as it is. Our standard-sized board was hot-glued to the back of an old standard-sized frame. You might just choose to prop your fabric-covered board on the wall. (Corkboard is available in standard sizes at craft suppliers, and can be cut to fit your frame if necessary.)

❧ COST: *$10 for board and fabric*   ❧ TIME: *30 minutes*   ❧ LEVEL: *1*   ❧ WHEN: *6 months to 1 year before the wedding.*

YOU WILL NEED

- ❧ *Tape measure*
- ❧ *Scissors*
- ❧ *Fabric to fit a board with an extra 3 inches added all around for folding under. One half yard of fabric is ample for most standard-sized bulletin boards.*
- ❧ *Corkboard (Try to find corkboard with cardboard backing or you can glue cardboard that has been cut to fit to the back of the corkboard so that staples will hold.)*

- ❧ *Stapler*
- ❧ *Glue gun*
- ❧ *Frame (optional)*
- ❧ *Stick pins*
- ❧ *Tiny bows or silk rose petals*

Cut fabric 3 inches larger than corkboard on all sides. Fold fabric over as shown, folding corners and trimming any excess fabric to remove bulk, then staple fabric to the back of the corkboard (you can also use a glue gun for this step). Using the glue gun, attach the board to the back of the frame or take it to a frame shop for installation.

Glue tiny ribbons and/or flower petals to the tops of stick pins.

Idea Book

A three-ring binder keeps all your wedding materials in one place, and like a file-o-fax, it is portable, so you can take it with you on shopping trips and to appointments with caterers and florists.

Use tab dividers to organize the binder according to topic, i.e., ceremony, reception, bridal and bridesmaid's gowns, flowers, etc. Reserve a section for magazine clippings so that you can easily show examples of styles you have in mind to others. Use a section as a journal so you have a place to write down experiences you would like to remember. Your average three-ring binder is not very romantic, but making the following cover from your choice of fabric will make it both lovely and useful.

COST: *About $15* ❧ TIME: *1 hour* ❧ LEVEL: *2* ❧ WHEN: *6 months to a year before the wedding*

- *Binder (11½ by 12 by 3 inches)*
- *Fabric (16½ by 36 inches)*
- *One 6-ounce package of 3mm pearls*
- *Beading thread*
- *Sewing needle*
- *Tape measure*
- *Scissors*
- *An iron*
- *Fusible web or glue*
- *1 yard of 2-inch-wide ribbon for tie to hold binder closed (optional)*

STEP 1. Measure the binder to be sure it is 11½ by 12 by 3 inches. Cut a 16½- by 36-inch rectangle of fabric. (Note: Cut the rectangle larger if your binder is bigger than the size recommended in these instructions. I suggest adding at least 4 inches to the binder size on the short ends and adding 2 inches on the long sides.)

Fold in the long sides 2 inches and press them with an iron. Hem the fabric with fusible web or glue. (Follow the fusible glue manufacturer's instructions.) We used fusible glue on this project. Fold the other ends in ½ inch and fuse them to hold the same way as the sides.

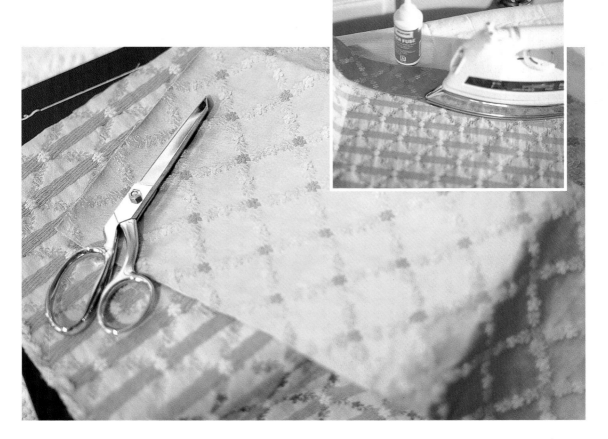

STEP 2. The next two steps explain how to add beading to the cover. Patterned or embroidered fabric lends itself to beading better than other fabric because you can use the pattern or embroidery design as a guide for where to put the beads. Set the binder on your fabric and fold the ends in, as shown in the top right photo, to check the fit and create a flap. Pin the flaps to hold.

STEP 3. Remove the cover and stitch the flaps closed on the right side of the fabric using tiny, overlapping stitches. (Slip a pearl on your thread with every stitch; repeat until the sides are closed.) Slip the cover on the binder once again and fold the other end for a nice snug fit. Pin to hold. Repeat the beading stitches for the other side flaps. Tack a 36-inch length of ribbon to the binder either with beaded stitches or by gluing it to the spine. Tie the ribbon in a bow to hold the binder closed. Trim the excess ribbon ends. Stitch beads or a ribbon rose (see page 47) on the spine for an extra touch of elegance.

Alternate Method

nstead of fabric glue, you can also use a sewing machine to make the cover. Use the same materials, but omit the beads and the rose. Measure the binder carefully, adding 2 inches on the sides for folding under, and 6 inches on the ends for the flaps. Fold the flap-ends ½-inch in, and stitch down. Fold the flap-end up over the end of the binder to mark it for a snug fit (about 5 inches). Mark the fabric with pins for stitching lines and stitch the flap sides. Repeat for the other end, adjusting the flap size for a nice snug fit. When you have stitched both flap ends, turn them right-side-out, and press them with an iron. Slip the cover on the binder, and make any necessary adjustments. The photo below shows how the cover looks on the outside when it is finished.

Make a bow-tie for the binding by folding a 5- by 9-inch rectangle of fabric. Stitch the sides, turn the fabric right-side-out, and pull out the corners with a pin or bone pointer. Press the sides with an iron. Fold and press a 3- by 6-inch rectangle of fabric. Wrap it around the bow and hand-stitch it to hold in the back of the bow. Hot-glue the finished bow to the spine of the binder.

Keep a calendar with envelope pockets in your binder. Write all appointments and important things to do in the calendar. Do not forget to post follow-up dates in the calendar, too.

Do-It-Yourself Wedding Stationery

Creating your own wedding announcements and invitations can be fun and easy. You can purchase everything you'll need at most office supply stores; in fact, some stores carry the supplies packaged as a kit. You can also buy precut ribbon and vellum overlays in a kit at your local office supply store. Who knew making one-of-kind stationery could be so easy?

Home computers provide a variety of fonts suitable for invitations, and if you have access to a scanner, the possibilities for adding patterns, texture, and imagery to your invitations is limitless. Glue strips of antique lace, ribbon, and dried flowers to the front of your cards to reflect the theme, season, or colors of your wedding. Handcrafted invitations are original and unforgettable!

Save-the-Date Cards

rint your "save-the-date" messages with the appropriate information from your computer. To make sure the message looks good on the size card you want to send, experiment with different fonts in different point sizes. When you are ready, you can print more than one message on a piece of 8½- x 11-inch paper (how many you can fit per page depends on the point size of your type).

YOU WILL NEED

- *Scissors or a paper cutter*
- *Decorative cardstock*
- *Colored stock or parchment paper*
- *Decorative papers*
- *Ribbon (two 6-inch-long, ¼-inch-wide pieces per card)*
- *Double-sided scotch tape*

Optional materials (all available at paper supply stores):
- *Stick-ons such as top hat and bow tie*
- *Hole punch*
- *Self-stick donut circles for reinforcing holes*
- *Small organza bag*
- *Gold paper hearts*

STEP 1. Precisely measure and cut two 4- by 6-inch rectangles of cardstock. Carefully cut a smaller rectangle (at least ⅛ of an inch smaller on each side) from the decorative paper. Brush a thin coat of craft glue to the back of the smaller rectangle and, making sure it is centered, press it glue-side-down to the rectangular piece of cardstock. Wait until the glue dries and the paper is securely adhered.

STEP 2. Print your save-the-date messages from your computer on parchment paper or nice marbled stock paper. Measure and cut each message in a rectangle measuring about 2½ by 3½ inches—that includes a border of about ¼ inch around the type. Attach the message to the card with double-sided scotch tape, making sure it is centered and firmly adhered.

STEP 3. Wrap the ribbon diagonally around the top left and bottom right corners of the card (see the photo below); tape the ends of the ribbon to the back of the card so that the ribbon is taut across the front. Finally, cover the ribbon ends by attaching the remaining 4- by 6-inch rectangle of cardstock to the back of the first card with double-sided scotch tape.

ALTERNATE IDEAS

TOP-HAT CARD. Follow the instructions for the ribbon card, but instead of attaching two pieces of ribbon to the corners, punch a hole in the top of the card with a hole puncher (the center of the hole should be about ½ inch from the top of the card). Stick a donut circle (or "hole reinforcer") over the hole, and tie a 6-inch length of ribbon in a bow through the hole. Place the stick-on top hat and bow tie to opposite sides of the message.

CONFETTI CARD. Print your save-the-date message from your computer on nice ivory or white stock paper. Measure and cut the message in a 2-inch by 2½-inch rectangle. Put the message in a small organza bag with little gold hearts, and tie the bag closed with a piece of ribbon (if it doesn't have a drawstring).

CHAPTER 3

Important Details from Head to Toe

No matter how dapper the groom looks, you can expect all eyes to be focused on the bride. If ever there were a time for gilding the lily, a wedding is it! Go over the top and indulge yourself in finery. This chapter will show you how to make yourself and your bridesmaids beautiful from head to toe without spending a fortune. Details such as ribbon and silk roses, handmade veils, satin bows and beaded trim for shoes, and rose wreaths give you a wealth of ideas for making the most of the day when you will be the center of attention. You can also adapt some of these details to use as decorations for table settings and other purposes.

Wedding Veils Made Easy

A bride's veil symbolizes a very old wedding tradition: in many different cultures, the bride's face is hidden until she stands at the altar, ready to exchange vows with her groom. In the early 1900's, many veils were made from silk illusion, which is very expensive and deteriorates over time. The material available today is made from synthetic fiber that will last indefinitely. To make your own wedding veil, you will need bridal netting, also known as tulle or bridal illusion. White and "candlelight" are the most popular colors. You can also find white tulle with an iridescent sheen, which is a lovely choice for evening weddings because it will sparkle in the soft lighting.

❧LENGTH: *Measure from the crown of your head to your waist—approximately 30 inches* ❧COST: *$9* ❧TIME: *1 hour or less* ❧LEVEL: *2* ❧WHEN: *2–3 months before the wedding*

YOU WILL NEED:

- 1 yard of 108-inch-wide tulle. (Tulle is available in two widths: 72 inches and 108 inches.) For longer veils, increase the yardage to the preferred length.
- 5 to 6 yards satin cording

- Needle and thread in color that matches tulle
- Sewing machine
- Scissors

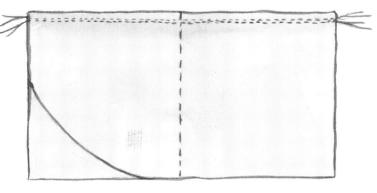

STEP 1. Cut the tulle 108 inches by 30 inches. Fold from the right to the left (see diagram) and cut a curve on the corners as shown.

STEP 2. Sew the cording with a straight stitch on your sewing machine, using a cording foot if you have one. You could use transparent mono-filament thread and sew the cording on with a zigzag stitch; however, the straight stitch gives a neater appearance. When you sew the cording, leave an edge of ½ inch of the tulle to the right of your stitching line. After you have finished stitching the cord to the tulle, trim this edge carefully with scissors as close to the cording as you can. It is not necessary to sew the cording to the top edge of the veiling.

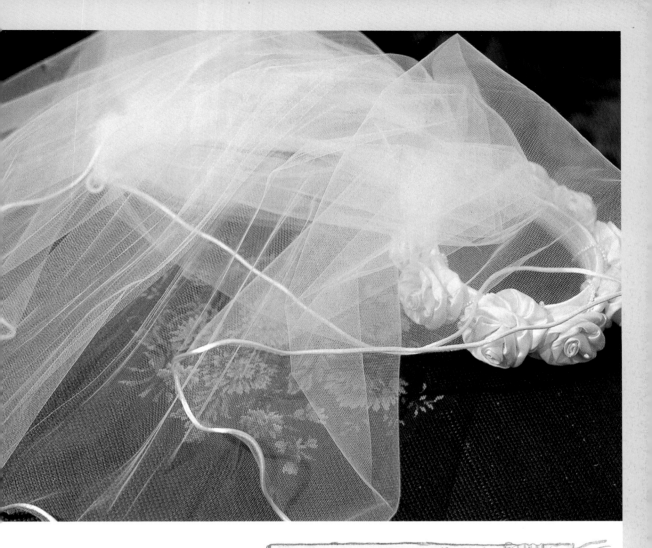

STEP 3. Sew two running gathering rows (see the stitch glossary on p. 9) at the top of the veil. Pull the threads gently to gather them (see diagram at right). When it is gathered, the top should measure about 4 inches. Using a sewing machine, sew back and forth across the gathers with a zigzag stitch to hold them in place. Trim all the threads and any raw edges of the netting. Make loops from the extra cording and stitch to the top of the gathers. Or, you can hand sew the veil to a small comb. The veil could also be stitched to the headband; however, most brides like to remove the veil after the ceremony.

Fabric Rose Bouquet

ake a fabric rose bouquet that your bridesmaids can keep or the bride
can toss. Select fabric that complements their dresses and gives them
unique, handcrafted detail. Hand-stitch the fabric roses (see instructions
on p. 46) to pipe cleaners, which will act as stems, and then wrap the pipe cleaners with
florist's tape. Gather the roses together and wrap with florist's tape once more, then wrap
the florist's tape with ribbon. If you like, you can also glue pearls in the center of each rose.

COST: *Approximately $10*   TIME: *2 hours*   LEVEL: *3*   WHEN: *2–3 months before wedding, especially if you want
to make several.*

YOU WILL NEED
(FOR ONE BOUQUET):

- Pipe cleaners (one package of 12)
- Fabric roses (6 or 7; see "Making Fabric Roses" on page 44)
- Needle and thread
- 3–4 yards of ½-inch-wide ribbon
- Craft glue
- Decorative pearls (one package of 48)
- Florist's tape
- Wire clippers

STEP 1. Stitch a pipe cleaner to the bottom of each rose. Stitch 12 inches of ribbon, folded to form loops, around each rose.

STEP 2. Gather the roses together by their wrapped pipe-cleaner stems and glue the rose heads to each other with a small dot of glue (the heads will be heavy, and the glue will help hold them close together). Dot each decorative pearl with glue, and stick about four pearls into the center of each rose. Firmly press the pearl into the fabric so that it adheres. Wrap florist's tape around the gathered stems, and cut off any ends that stick out with the wire clippers. Wrap over the florist's tape with ribbon, and then tie the bouquet with a pretty bow.

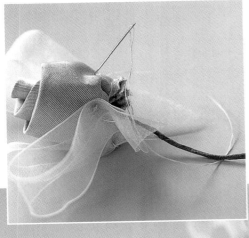

Making Fabric Roses

abric roses add gorgeous decorative detail to tables, pews, bridal dresses, and veils. To make them, it's best to use satin, lace, organdy, or tulle.

When you cut the material to size, it will have a raw edge. To hide that edge and to form the shape of the rose, you must first fold the fabric so the raw edges are at one side and then gather the raw edge, rolling and tacking to form the rose.

Note: If you are working with an antique piece of fabric, you'll want to make smaller roses to get the most out of your material.

COST: *$.25–.50 each* ❦ TIME: *1–2 minutes* ❦ LEVEL: *2* ❦ TIME: *Several months before the wedding*

YOU WILL NEED
(FOR 20 ROSES):

- *½ yard of fabric such as satin, organza, crepe, tulle, or lace*
- *Needle and thread (in a color that matches the fabric)*

five turns to form the center of rose. With a needle and thread, sew four or five gathering stitches (see stitch glossary on p. 9), pull to gather, then tack to the back of the rose center with a stitch or two.

STEP 1. Cut a 3- by 24-inch strip of fabric on the bias.

STEP 2. Double-thread the sewing needle, knot the end, and put the needle aside. Fold the fabric strip in half lengthwise (so it's 1½ by 24 inches) with the right side (meaning the side of the fabric you want showing) facing out. Tightly roll the end of the folded fabric in four or

STEP 3. Continue gathering and stitching until the rose is formed. Sew the end of the fabric to the back of the rose.

Making Ribbon Roses

ake these versatile ribbon roses for headbands, corsages, and to accent your bridal dress. Once you master the basic technique, you can branch out and experiment with different sizes and kinds of ribbon. (The width and length of the ribbon you use will determine the size of the rose.) Any ribbon you choose, whether wired or soft and silky, will produce a unique and lovely rose.

COST PER ROSE: *$.25–.50*

TIME: *1–2 minutes*   LEVEL: *2*

DO: *Several months before the wedding*

YOU WILL NEED

- *Ribbon (at least a 12-inch length per rose)*
- *Needle and thread*
- *Scissors*

STEP 1. For a 2-inch rose, cut a length of ribbon approximately 12 inches long by 1½ inches wide. Double thread the needle, knot the end, and set it aside. Turn one end of the ribbon down, and then roll four or five turns to form the center of the rose. With your left hand, hold the center in place and secure it with a couple of stitches.

STEP 2. Turn the ribbon with a twist and tack it with a stitch or two to hold. Turn it again, then twist and stitch. (You are shaping the rose as you continue the process.) Repeat until you come to the end of the ribbon. Tack the end of the ribbon to the bottom of the rose. If the rose does not look satisfactory, it's easy to take the stitches out and start over.

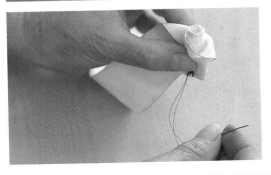

Ribbon Rose Headband

A bride's headdress can be as simple as a single flower artfully placed or as elaborate as a tiara or a crown of roses. The base for this pretty rose hair accessory is a satin headband available at most wedding fabric stores. Make the ribbon roses on page 45 and simply glue or sew them to the headband. You can attach an organza veil with beautiful cording to make the headdress more romantic and formal, or simply wear it alone to keep curls or a special hairstyle in place.

❧COST: *Approximately $15* ❧TIME: *2–3 hours* ❧LEVEL: *2* ❧DO: *At least 2 months before the wedding*

YOU WILL NEED

- ❧ *Satin roses (7)*
- ❧ *Satin headband*
- ❧ *Glue gun*
- ❧ *Sewing needle*
- ❧ *Thread to match fabric*

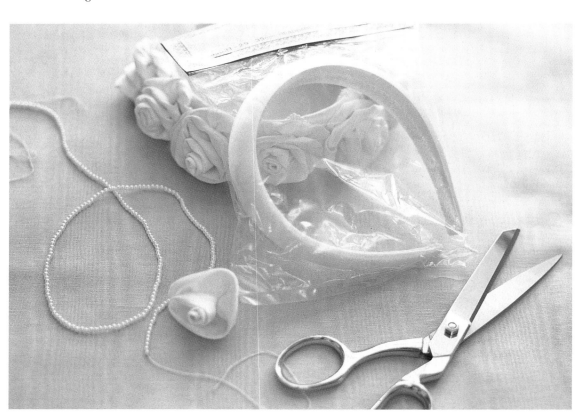

STEP 1. Make seven 2-inch-wide ribbon roses. (Instructions on page 47.)

STEP 2. Sew the roses to the headband with hand stitches or attach them with a glue gun. I prefer to hand-stitch the roses so I can curve them around the headband by tacking them with little stitches under each. Then I don't need to worry about glue dripping and marking the satin. However, if you are careful about watching where the glue goes, using the glue gun is easier than sewing.

Crown of Roses

or an outdoor or rustic ceremony, it's hard to imagine anything more charming than the bride and bridesmaids wearing these delicate crowns of roses in their hair. The small silk roses are available at most craft supply stores packaged in bundles with the stems held together with a twisty. The bundles can be pulled apart, and each rose has a wire attached that makes wrapping it around a garland quite simple. The large silk roses fill out the wreath and give it lovely color. Make these wreaths for the bride and bridesmaids, flower girls, or even to use as table decorations.

COST: *About $15*   TIME: *1 hour or less*   LEVEL: *1*   DO: *2–3 months before the wedding*

YOU WILL NEED (FOR ONE CROWN):

- *30 inches of leaf garland (available, along with the roses, at most craft supply stores)*
- *12 tiny roses with wire stems*
- *5 large artificial roses*
- *3–4 yards of ¼-inch-wide ribbon*
- *Glue gun*

STEP 1. Measure around your head in the exact place where you want the crown to sit, and then add 6 inches. Measure and cut the garland to that length (the total length should be in the ballpark of 22 to 23 inches).

STEP 2. Wrap the wire stem of each small rose around the garland between the leaves, spacing the roses about 1 inch apart. When you are finished, you can bend the leaves to frame your roses and cover any unsightly wires. Twist the ends of the garland together to form a circle. Tie the ribbon streamers to the closed ends of the garland in a delicate bow.

STEP 3. Using the glue gun, apply glue to the backs of the larger roses, and firmly press them to the garland at appropriate places around the crown. Use enough glue to hold the roses, but don't use so much that it drips or stains the smaller flowers.

Updating an Heirloom Gown

ou may have a beautiful vintage gown that's a little worse for the wear. Or it
may be your dream to get married in your mother or grandmother's wedding
dress, but the style is dated and it just doesn't fit. Don't worry—an antique
gown or one that is cut simply can be updated and transformed by an experienced seamstress. You can then add beautiful details and accents by simply pinning a few satin roses to
the waist or sleeve of the dress. Here are some ideas for making an heirloom wedding dress
look beautiful. After the dress has been hemmed and altered for fit, have it professionally
cleaned and pressed—and voilá! Everything old is indeed new again.

☙COST: *Cost of professional alterations, cleaning, and pressing* ☙TIME: *A weekend* ☙LEVEL: *Unless you are very skilled at*
dressmaking, you will need to hire an experienced seamstress to do this project. ☙DO: *At least 6 months before the wedding*

FOR A VERY EXPERIENCED OR PROFESSIONAL SEAMSTRESS

If your vintage dress has a long train that is either damaged or whose style doesn't suit you, you can trim some fabric off to provide a nice, curved, sweep-length train. You can use the trimmed-off fabric to make a simple bustle and three roses and then float the bustle and roses on a veil of tulle with satin ribbon trim. Sew hooks on the bustle to attach it to your dress. Or, if you like, you can make a new train from appropriately measured tulle (the length is up to you) and sew satin ribbon to the edges.

DRESSING UP A SIMPLE DRESS

Unless you are an experienced seamstress with knowledge of bridal fabrics and dress design, I don't recommend that you undertake making your own wedding dress—it's best to leave that to a professional. You can, however, add details to an off-the-rack dress by simply pinning silk roses to the waist or sleeve. The combined effect of the silk roses on your dress and the rose headband (p. 48) or the rose crown (p. 50) in your hair will be romantic and enchanting, especially if they complement the flowers in your bouquet!

Satin Shoe Bows

Opting for comfort over style is smart when you're choosing shoes for your wedding. There are plenty of ways to make a comfortable pair of shoes look gorgeous. Hunt in antique shops, for instance, for antique shoe clips you can attach to delicate flats. Another good idea is to shop for ready-made lace appliqués that you can glue to a simple shoe for a graceful, classic look. Bows of simple satin ribbon can also gussy up otherwise sober feet.

Note: Several weeks before the wedding, wear your shoes around the house a few times to break them in.

❧COST: *Approximately $15* ❧TIME: *About 2 hours* ❧LEVEL: *3* ❧WHEN: *2 months before the wedding*

- *One pair of simple closed-toe shoes*
- *Satin fabric (⅛ of a yard)*
- *Tape measure*
- *Scissors*
- *Iron*
- *Straight pins*

- *Sewing needle and thread*
- *Pearl-beaded buttons (2)*
- *Glue gun*
- *14 inches of beaded trim, pearls, or pearl strands (for shoes with straps only)*

STEP 1. To make the "leaf" bows, cut four rectangles of satin fabric measuring 4 inches by 8 inches each. Fold the length of the 8-inch side down ½ inch and press with the iron. Place your finger in the center of the 8-inch side and fold each outer, upper corner of the rectangle in one at a time, smoothing and pinning the edges (see photo below). You should now have a triangle, or leaf. Gather the bottom with sewing thread and needle (see photo), and tack it to hold it in place. (Repeat for the remaining three rectangles of fabric.)

STEP 2. Tack two "leaves" together with needle and thread at their raw edges and stitch a button over the center. (Repeat for the other two leaves.)

STEP 3. Using a glue gun, attach one complete leaf bow to each shoe. Tack the bow at the sides so that it follows the curve of the top of the shoe.

STEP 4. If the shoes have straps, glue beaded or pearl trim to the actual strap. Do not glue the beaded trim over an elastic strap.

Lace Appliqué Shoe Details

Decorate your shoes with lace appliqués, which are available at wedding fabric stores. Suitable lace with cording around each floral or geometric design such as Alençon lace (a delicate, needlepoint lace) is also available by the yard. This cording prevents the lace from fraying when it's cut and provides a nice finished edge and frame for each motif in the pattern. (Alençon lace is most often recognized as embellishment for wedding bodices and hems.) To determine the proper amount of lace to purchase, study the pattern in the lace yardage to make sure that you have at least three motif sections you can separate by careful snipping with small scissors. Arranging three motifs around the shoe opening creates a pleasing border. About an 8-inch length of 3-inch wide Alençon lace trim will do nicely for this project.

COST: *About $11* TIME: *Less than 1 hour* LEVEL: *1* DO: *2 months before the wedding*

YOU WILL NEED

- *2 ready-made appliqués of your choice, or 6 to 8 inches of Alencon lace trim*
- *Glue gun*
- *Scissors*
- *12 inches of 1½-inch-wide wired-satin ribbon (optional)*

STEP 1. If you select ready-made appliqués, set them aside—no preparation is required, they are ready to glue on. If you select Alençon lace trim, clip carefully around the appliqué shapes—there are usually three (two should be symmetrical)—so that the design will curve nicely around the mouth of the shoe.

STEP 2. Fold the wired ribbon in two loops. Tack the ends of the loops with pins to hold them, and then, using the glue gun, glue the ends together. Press down so that the edges are firmly stuck together. Remove the pins, and then glue the raw edge of the folded loops to the mouth of shoe (see photo). Glue the ready-made or cut lace appliqués to the raw edge of the ribbon so that they curve around and cover it.

Gifts for the Wedding Party

Bridesmaids and groomsmen are an integral part of every traditional wedding party, as are flower girls and ring bearers. They become like an extended family, sharing the anxiety and happiness of this big event in your life. Show your "extended" and immediate family how much you appreciate them being there with small, individual gifts. If you don't want to worry about picking something to suit each person's unique taste, go with fail-safe gift choices such as earrings or a simple necklace for your bridesmaids and cufflinks or bowties for the groomsmen. You can make your gifts more personal by presenting them in lovely boxes and wrappings made with old jewelry, ribbons, and whimsical objects. If you have the time and energy, make your bridesmaids and perhaps the mothers of the bride and groom a beaded purse—they will be touched by the gesture. This chapter is full of many other ideas for giving your loved ones personal, handcrafted tokens of your thanks.

Beaded Purses

ake this beaded purse to complement the color of the bride and bridesmaid's gowns. It will come in handy for carrying essential items on the
wedding day and makes an elegant evening bag for future nights out.
Embroidered silk is ideal for beadwork because you can place the beads along the design of
the embroidery. Two layers of fabric sewn together like a pillowcase, turned right-side-out,
and stuffed with low-loft quilt batting automatically become quilted and give the purse
body when you bead it. Use pretty buttons, tassels, and rosettes as finishing touches.

COST PER ROSE: *Approximately $20*　TIME: *2–3 hours*　LEVEL: *2*　DO: *A few weeks before the wedding*

YOU WILL NEED

- *Tape measure*
- *10- by 36-inch piece of silk fabric with repeat all-over embroidered pattern*
- *9- by 18-inch piece of low-loft quilt batting*
- *Straight pins*
- *Sewing thread to match silk*
- *Sewing needle*
- *4 small binder clips*
- *Sewing machine*

- *30 gram package of 3mm pearls (or other beads in size of your choice)*
- *Beading thread*
- *Velcro circles or snap for closure*

OPTIONAL MATERIALS:

- *18 inches of braid or cording for handle*
- *Scotch tape*
- *6 inches of 1½-inch-wide satin ribbon for bow*
- *1-inch pearl button*

STEP 1. Take the 10- by 36-inch piece of silk fabric and, with the embroidered side facing in, fold it in half in a 10- by 18-inch rectangle. Making sure the unpatterned side is facing out, pin and then sew three sides closed (remove the pins as you sew). Leave one of the 10-inch ends of the rectangle open. Clip the corners, turn the fabric right-side-out, and press the edges flat with your fingers. You may use an iron if you like, but do so carefully—you don't want to burn the material. For neat corners, pull them out with a pin. You should now have what looks like a long, narrow pillowcase. Take the 9- by 18-inch piece of quilt batting and put it inside the "pillowcase," making sure the corners are filled. Tuck the open end of the fabric inside ½ inch, and pin it. Using a sewing machine, stitch the end closed, removing the pins as you go. You can also stitch it closed by hand using a slip-stitch or tiny overlapping stitches (see stitch glossary on p. 9), again, removing the pins as you go.

STEP 2. You are now ready to bead the bag. Fill a dish with beads so that they are easy to pick up. Thread your needle with a beading thread, knot it, and sew one pearl over the center of each "repeat pattern" in the embroidery. You can sew beads in other places, too, but just make sure your work looks symmetrical rather than haphazard. Trim any traveling thread ends on the lining side when you are finished.

STEP 3. When you are finished beading, fold the end of the finished rectangle over by a little more than a third of its length (about 7 inches). That fold creates the pouch of the bag, and the roughly 4 inches of remaining material will be the flap that folds over to close the bag. Smooth the folded bottom edge of the bag with your fingertips, and stitch the sides closed with a sewing machine or by hand. Fold the top of the bag over, and sew the Velcro circles on the inside of the flap and the front of the bag so that they meet and hold the purse closed.

IDEAS FOR FINISHING TOUCHES

CORDED STRAP. Choose whatever length strap you like. Make a circle of Scotch tape in the center of the piece of braid or cord, then wind the 1½-inch-wide ribbon over the tape and secure it to the cord with hand stitches. Stitch the cord to the inside of the purse.

SATIN BOW ACCENT. Make a satin bow according to the instructions for "Satin Shoe-Bows" on p. 54. Tack the finished bow to the flap of the purse with hand stitches, or use a glue gun.

Gift Ideas

Don't overlook the groomsmen! They may not want anything frilly or pretty, but you can use your imagination to present thoughtful gifts with a personal touch.

- Why not give each groomsman a nice bow tie to wear at the wedding? Wrap the tie around a small pillow or a bottle of scotch, and attach a card with how-to-tie instructions. (See p. 68 for instructions on hand-sewing a pillow, but substitute plaid or solid-color fabric for the lace.)

- Gift wrap a set of golf balls and attach a "bouquet" of tee's tied together with ribbon to the gift box.

- Give each groomsman a custom-mono-grammed baseball cap with ribbon-wrapped tickets to a special sports event tucked inside.

Jeweled Gift Boxes

The wrapping can be as much of a gift as what's inside with these exquisite jeweled gift boxes. They are distinctive, easy to do, and all you need are the boxes, some pretty ribbons, and some pieces of inexpensive costume jewelery or whatever unmatched or broken odds and ends you can find in your jewelry box. If you have some scraps of old lace and pieces of ribbon, use them too! You can even use ornaments such as pretty buttons, dried flowers, or small silk birds to decorate the boxes; these are easy to find at gift wrap and paper supply stores.

❧COST: *Approximately $1.50 per box*   ❧TIME: *10–15 minutes*   ❧LEVEL: *1*   ❧DO: *Anytime before the wedding*

- ❧ *An assortment of silver or gold gift boxes*
- ❧ *6-inch lengths of ribbon such as brocades, floral appliqué, or tapestry*
- ❧ *Scissors*
- ❧ *Glue gun*
- ❧ *Odd pieces of jewelry such as earrings, brooches, or stones and beads from necklaces*
- ❧ *Silk leaves and flowers, pretty buttons, silk birds, or other ornaments*

Trim the boxes with the lengths of ribbon, using the glue gun to adhere them. You can attach the ribbon to the lid of the box, around its sides, or completely cover it. Then take the odd pieces of jewelry and/or the buttons and glue them as accents over the ribbons. You can make each box differ-ent—use different colors of ribbon, different jewels, or cover the box with silk leaves and flowers. Simple or intricate, the design is up to you. It really is better to give than receive, and this project makes it a lot more fun!

FOR THE GUESTS
Sachets

ive each of your wedding guests one of these sweet sachets as a fragrant keepsake. You can make them from scraps of antique fabric, or you can take a trip to the fabric store and find an array of gorgeous fabric remnants to use. Use your favorite dusting powder to give the pillows a touch of delicate scent (essential oils or sachet fillers can be overpowering). Finish by adding tassels, rosettes, beads, or other trims to make these mementos even more precious.

❧COST: *About $2 each* ❧TIME: *About ½ hour each* ❧LEVEL: *1* ❧DO: *Anytime before the wedding*

- *Scissors*
- *Tape measure*
- *2 squares of 5- by 5-inch fabric for each pillow*
- *Pins*
- *Needle and thread or sewing machine*
- *Bag of poly stuffing large enough to make enough pillows for your guests*
- *Dusting powder*
- *An assortment of tassels, rosettes, and/or beads*

STEP 1. Cut two 5- by 5-inch squares of fabric. With the right sides (the sides you want to show) together, sew around the edges of the square, leaving a three-inch opening at the top side.

STEP 2. Turn the square right-side-out, and pull the corners out with a pin. Sprinkle a small amount of dusting powder on enough of the poly stuffing to fill the pillow. Stuff the fabric with the poly-fill and stitch the opening closed with tiny overlapping stitches.

STEP 3. Hand-stitch the tassels, rosettes, and/or beads to the edges of the pillow and ta da! Your one-of-a-kind sachet is done.

FOR THE LITTLE ONES
A Little Something

Even the junior wedding party members deserve a fun gift. Why not give them a stuffed animal such as a mouse, bear, or bunny dressed in wedding attire? They'll have something to play with during the wedding (which could be a blessing) and take home. Go to a toy store and pick out some cute and expressive stuffed animals. Then all you really need to make the stuffed animal bride and groom are scraps of lace and jewelry and a simple bow tie.

COST: *$8–$15*   TIME: *A few minutes*   LEVEL: *1*   DO: *At least 1 month before the wedding*

YOU WILL NEED

- Stuffed animals
- Scraps of lace
- Scraps of rhinestone jewelry
- Glue gun
- Bow tie
- Needle and thread (optional)
- Doll dress (optional)

If you have a suitable white doll's dress, slip this on one of the stuffed animals. If you don't, just wrap a piece of lace around the animal's waist and secure it with the glue gun to make a lace skirt. Decorate the neckline with an old earring or brooch. Glue a scrap of net to the animal's head for an impromptu veil and top it with a piece of junk jewelry for a headdress. For the stuffed animal groom, all you need to do is attach a bow tie in the appropriate place with a glue gun.

CHAPTER 5

Showers of Happiness

The term bridal shower refers to an old custom: Party guests would fill an upside-down umbrella with gifts and then turn it over for a literal shower of good wishes for the bride-to-be. Nowadays, the bridal shower is a time for friends and close family members to give the bride fun gifts and share their best wishes in an intimate setting. Theme showers such as linen, kitchen-ware and recipe, or lingerie parties are becoming more and more common. The guests know what to bring and the bride gets an ample supply of something she may not have. If you are hosting a shower, the projects in this chapter will show you how to make everything from your invitations to your table settings beautiful and special.

Bridal Shower Invitations

A shower invitation packaged in a silver box dressed with a pretty petticoat is perfect for a lingerie party. The box is filled with confetti, along with information about the date, time, and location of the party, who to call to RSVP, and suggestions for gifts. This unusual invitation won't sit on anyone's desk unnoticed—the confetti will give your guests plenty of little reminders to pick up off the floor for days. Mail the little box in a padded envelope to protect it from damage, and check with your post office to determine the proper postage.

COST: *Approximately $1–$2 each* TIME: *45 minutes* LEVEL: *1* DO: *2 weeks before the shower*

YOU WILL NEED
(FOR 20 INVITATIONS):

- Scissors
- Netting or scrim for skirts (½ yard)
- Ribbon (3 yards long, ¼ inch wide) for sashes
- Ribbon (3½ yards long, 1 inch wide) for box wrap
- Construction paper for bodice
- Double-sided tape
- Glue gun
- One 60-gram tube of 2mm craft beads (Rocailles)
- Tiny flowers, ribbon rosettes, or bows for sash trim
- 4- by 4-inch square silver boxes (20)
- Pencil
- Tape measure
- Confetti
- Printed invitations with shower information
- 20 padded envelopes for mailing
- Appropriate postage

STEP 1. Cut twenty 2- by 5-inch rectangles of net/scrim for the skirts, twenty 2-inch-long, ¼-inch-wide pieces of ribbon for the sashes, and twenty 6-inch-long pieces of ribbon to wrap around the boxes. Then use the template (opposite) to cut 20 construction paper bodices. Sew gathering stitches along one 5-inch side of each net rectangle; gather the stitches so that the material bunches to fit the width of the bodice. Set the netting aside.

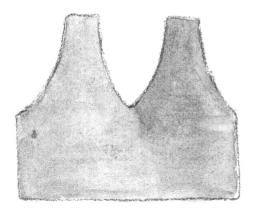

BRIDAL SHOWER IDEA

Plan a linen party for your backyard, porch, or garden. Have the guests hang their gifts (i.e. sheets, pillowcases, hand towels, etc.), on the clothesline. You will have instant party decorations! You could also tack up temporary clotheslines in your living room for an indoor party.

STEP 2. With double-sided tape or a glue gun, attach the 6-inch piece of ribbon in a band around the middle of the box lid. Tape the netting to the bottom edge of the bodice, making sure it is even and well adhered. Then glue the 2-inch-long ribbon sash on the bodice, tucking the ends under, and glue the bodice to the ribbon-band on the box lid. Finally, glue the beads, flowers, rosettes, etc., to the sash.

STEP 3. When the glue is dry, fill the box with a small amount of confetti and the shower instructions. Tuck the box into a padded envelope and mail it with the appropriate postage.

Teacup Bouquets

A small bouquet in a delicate china cup at each place setting is perfect for a bridal shower. It is pretty and colorful and best of all—it is easy to make. Look for old or odd teacups at tag sales if you don't have any of your own.

They don't have to be perfect; a little chip or two will not show when the cups are filled with flowers. If you don't want to invest in more than a few teacups or if you aren't having a sit-down shower, use a group of three or five to decorate a gift or dessert table.

🐦COST: *About $2 per favor* 🐦 TIME: *A few minutes* 🐦LEVEL: *1* 🐦DO: *The night before or morning of the shower*

YOU WILL NEED
(FOR ONE BOUQUET):

- 🐦 *One china teacup*
- 🐦 *Floral foam*
- 🐦 *Knife*
- 🐦 *Water*
- 🐦 *Scissors*
- 🐦 *Small bunch of flowers such as spray roses, daisies, baby's breath, violets, and pansies*

- 🐦 *Glue gun*
- 🐦 *Sprigs of dried flowers such as lavender*
- 🐦 *Plain name tags on a string (available at stationery stores)*

STEP 1. With a knife, cut a chunk of floral foam a little larger than the diameter of your cup so that it fits snugly inside. When you're using the knife, be sure to cut in the direction *away from* your body so that you don't cut yourself if your hand slips. Pour just enough water on the foam to wet it thoroughly. Pour off any excess water.

STEP 2. Trim the stems of the flowers so that they are about the height of the teacup. Push the flower stems into the foam. Start by putting the larger flowers, such as roses, in the center and fill in and around the large blooms with smaller flowers and leaves. Be sure that you use enough flowers to cover all the foam. If you make them the night before the shower, keep the finished bouquets in your refrigerator overnight so they stay fresh.

STEP 3. Write each guest's name on a name tag. Glue a border of dried flowers around each tag, and either tie it around a napkin or to the handle of a teacup bouquet if have made one for each place setting.

OTHER SIMPLE CENTER-PIECES

A centerpiece for your bridal shower can be a simple grouping of little crystal vases or even old salt shakers. Look around the house for little vases, jars, or other containers that can be arranged in a grouping with deli-cate flowers. Tag sales, flea markets, and antique shops are good places to find unique salt shakers without spending a lot.

Bridal Garter

The tradition of the groom tossing the bride's garter to a group of unmarried male guests evolved from an even older tradition: It was once customary for the wedding guests to sit on the bride and groom's bed and help them remove their stockings—the men removed the bride's and the ladies removed the groom's. Then they would fling the stockings over their shoulders: If a lady hit the groom, she was the next to be married, and the same was true for a man whose stocking hit the bride. Luckily, this custom is now much simpler and less intrusive. Make this pretty garter with blue ribbon—even if you don't do a garter-toss, the bride will have her indispensable "something blue."

☙COST: *$5* ☙ TIME:*1 hour* ☙LEVEL: *2* ☙DO: *1 month before the wedding*

- 2½ yards of 1-inch-wide blue ribbon
- Sewing machine
- 1 yard of 2-inch-wide white ribbon
- 1 yard beaded fringe trim
- 1 yard of ¾-inch-wide soft elastic
- Small safety pin
- 4 inches of 1-inch-wide blue ribbon

- for bow
- One rhinestone button
- Sewing needle and thread to match garter
- Scissors
- Tape measure
- Straight pins

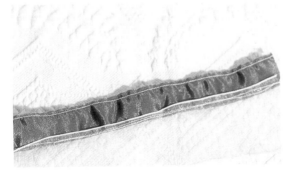

STEP 1. Using the sewing machine, sew two edges of two layers of blue ribbon together to make a casing for the elastic (see top photo). Then sew the length of the piece of white ribbon along the edge of the blue ribbon-casing.

STEP 2. Take the beaded trim and sew it over the seam where the blue and white ribbons are joined (see bottom photo).

STEP 3. Thread the piece of elastic into the blue casing using a safety pin to help guide it along. Pull the elastic to gather the garter so it will fit comfortably; a length of about 12 inches should be sufficient.

STEP 4. Tie the extra piece of blue ribbon into a bow and sew it where the ends of the garter join together. Sew a rhinestone button in the center of the bow.

Fresh Flower Pillows

A tiny lace pillow with a pocket for a name tag and a small sprig of fresh flowers makes an adorable present to give each of the shower guests. The pillows are similar to sachets, but fresh flowers are the only scented thing about these. Look for small, antique square-lace medallions at a flea market or buy new ones at a bridal fabric store. The rest of the pillow is made from scrim (cotton netting) and poly-fill stuffing. It's fine to use such fabric as satin, cotton, or silk instead, but scrim netting is inexpensive, handles well, and has a light, airy look.

COST: *About $2 each*   TIME: *About 15–20 minutes*   LEVEL: *2*   DO: *Several months before the wedding*

YOU WILL NEED (PER PILLOW):

- Scissors
- Tape measure
- One 4- by 8-inch rectangle of scrim (½ yard of scrim makes approximately 24 pillows)
- Sewing machine
- Poly stuffing
- 4- by 4-inch lace medallion squares or circles
- Thread to match fabric and sewing needle
- Straight pins

STEP 1. Cut a 4- by 8-inch rectangle of scrim. Fold it in half to make a 4-inch square. Sew three sides, leaving one end open. Turn the material right-side-out, and stuff enough poly filling in the opening to the pillow plump but not overstuffed. Hand-sew the open end closed with tiny overlapping stitches.

STEP 2. Hand-stitch three sides of a lace medallion to the finished pillow, but leave the top side open to make a pocket. Tuck a small sprig of fresh flowers in the pocket with a little name tag or message. Put one flower pillow at each place setting, or put them in a pretty basket or bowl and give one to each guest after the bride has opened all her shower gifts.

The Big Day

The big day has finally arrived. You've completed all the preparations, and now you're ready for all the excitement to unfold. All day people will be scurrying about taking care of last minute details, you'll be surrounded by family and friends, and your nerves may be frazzled, but it's time to take a deep breath and enjoy all of your hard work. The projects in this chapter will show you ways to add your personal touch to everything from decorations for the ceremony and reception to favor boxes and toasting glasses—you even have a "wedding emergency box" at hand in anticipation of missing buttons or snagged stockings. You have planned carefully, delegated responsibility, and prepared for emergencies. Now let yourself relax and savor the joy of each moment.

PROJECTS FOR
THE CEREMONY

Wedding Emergency Kit

Ceremony Decorations:
Taffeta Bows
Satin Bows
Beaded Bows

Flower Girl's Basket

Ringbearer's Pillows:
Beaded Silk Pillow
Antique Lace Pillow

Wedding Emergency Kit

ake this lovely, decorated box to hold all the emergency items you may need on your wedding day. If you get a run in your stockings, catch your heel in your dress hem, or need to sew on a renegade button, don't panic—you have your emergency kit! You can get a cardboard box with a hinged lid at most craft supply stores. All you have to do is embellish it with fabric and pretty trims. When you no longer need it, pass it on to a friend who is getting married soon. Here are some essentials with which you should stock the box.

❧COST: *Approximately $20*   ❧ TIME: *About 2 hours*   ❧LEVEL: *2*   ❧DO: *Several months before the wedding*

- Scissors
- Tape measure
- Sturdy box (10 by 12 inches) with a lid
- Piece of fabric—about 12 by 18 inches
- Sewing machine
- Needle and thread

- Glue gun
- Beaded lace trim—about 24 inches
- Braid trim—at least 2 yards
- Ribbon trim—at least 1 yard
- 18-inch length of tulle ribbon for bow (optional)

STEP 1. Cut the fabric for the top of the box 2 inches wider and 6 inches longer than the lid so that you can tuck the edges under and so you can accommodate the gathers you will make. (Our box was 10 by 12 inches.) By hand or with a sewing machine, sew running stitches down the center of the fabric and at two ends. Pull the stitches to gather the fabric within 1 inch of the lid size, leaving the 1 inch for turning under.

STEP 2. Glue the gathered fabric to the lid with the glue gun, and turn the raw ends under the lid. Glue the trims over the gathering stitches.

STEP 3. Glue the trims to the sides of the box. If you desire, you can tack extra wedding gown buttons to the box lid. For the crowning touch, wrap the finished box with a tulle bow.

EMERGENCY KIT CONTENTS

Extra nylons
Comb
Lipstick and/or lip gloss
Clear fingernail polish
Sewing thread in
appropriate colors
Safety pins
Breath mints
Buttons
Handkerchief or tissues
Hairspray
Pen/pencil
Aspirin/ibuprofen
Hair pins
Scissors
Watch
Mirror
Toothpaste/toothbrush
Hem tape
Dental floss

Creating Decorative Bows

Once you master making fabric bows, there will be no end to the wonderful detail you can add to your wedding decorations. You can use them to embellish a wedding gown with detail at the back waist or to adorn a flower girl's dress. Bows are less expensive to make with fabric than they are with ready-made ribbon. They take very little time, and most "weekend seamstresses" can master them without much trouble. Experiment with a range of different fabrics and embellish them with beadwork and flowers. We will show you how to make three different kinds of bows: a crisp taffeta bow, a satin bow, and a beaded embroidered silk bow. You can use them to decorate the chairs and aisles at your ceremony site, the tables at your reception, or as details for bride and bridesmaids' gowns. The only limit is your imagination!

Taffeta Bow

ake these pretty bows to decorate the chairs or pews at the ceremony site, or to decorate the doorway as a wedding welcome for your guests. Add a few fresh flowers as accents to make the decoration even more dramatic. These bows look lovely as accents for outdoor weddings: place them on tables, gazebo railings, trellises, or garden gates.

COST: *$10 per bow*   TIME: *1 hour*   LEVEL: *2*   WHEN: *2–4 months prior to the wedding date, especially if you want to use lots of bows.*

YOU WILL NEED

- Scissors
- Tape measure
- ½ yard of taffeta fabric
- Iron
- Thread to match fabric and sewing needle
- Straight pins

- Sewing machine
- 4 yards of wired satin ribbon 1 ½ inches wide
- Florist's wire (optional)
- Fresh flowers (optional)

STEP 1. Cut three 12- by 30-inch rectangles of taffeta. Fold each in half to make a 6- by 30-inch rectangle. Sew down the long sides and across one end. Turn the fabric right-side-out, and pull the corners out with a pin for a neat finish. Lightly press the fabric with an iron. Repeat this process for the other two rectangles.

STEP 2. Fold the raw, open edge of the rectangle end down 6 inches, then pin it and sew two rows of running, gathering stitches across it. Pull the threads to gather them. Repeat this step for the other two rectangles.

STEP 3. Layer the three pieces of taffeta and sew them together along the rows of gathering stitches. Puff out the three loops at the top of the sewn-together pieces of fabric, and firmly fold the top loop down; it will then become the bottom loop of a bow (the top loop is formed by the loop of the second layer of taffeta). Take the yard of wired satin ribbon and fold it in half. Using the needle and thread, tack the ribbon at the folded down loop. Fold sections of the ribbon up one at a time to form about three more same-size loops. Tack them with the needle and thread, and stitch the loops of wired ribbon to the center of the taffeta bow. You can wire or hot-glue fresh or silk flowers to the center of the bows on the morning of the ceremony if you like.

Satin and Tulle Bows

❧ COST: *Approximately $5 per bow*
❧ TIME: *1 hour*
❧ LEVEL: *2*
❧ DO: *3–4 months before the wedding,*
especially if you have several to make.

YOU WILL NEED
(FOR ONE BOW):

- ✀ *3 fabric roses (see p. 46)*
- ✀ *Scissors*
- ✀ *Tape measure*
- ✀ *Satin fabric (⅓ yard per bow)*
- ✀ *Straight pins*
- ✀ *Sewing thread to match ribbon and sewing needle*
- ✀ *Sewing machine*
- ✀ *Satin ribbon (2 yards, 1½ inches wide)*
- ✀ *Tulle (½ yard, 108 inches wide)*
- ✀ *Satin ribbon—4 yards, ¼ inch wide for streamers (optional)*
- ✀ *Cording (18 inches) or ribbon (18 inches ¼ inch wide) for tie*

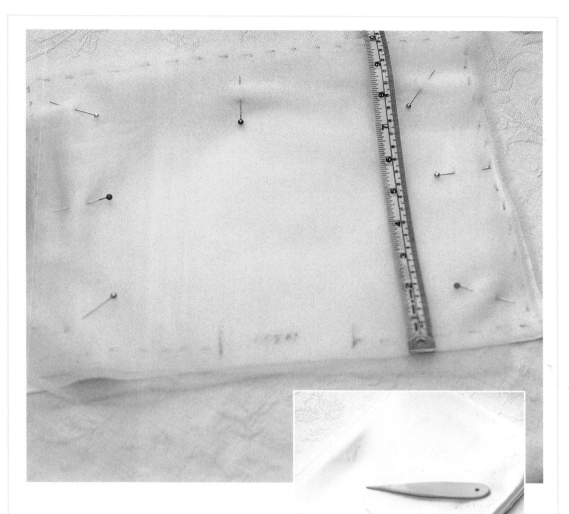

STEP 1. Make three 2-inch diameter fabric roses for each bow (see p. 46 for instructions).

STEP 2. Cut two rectangles of satin measuring 10 by 12 inches. Cut eight 10-by 12-inch layers of tulle. Put both rectangles of satin together wrong-side-out. Pin the eight layers of tulle to the satin rectangle and stitch all the layers together on three sides, leaving an opening of three inches at one end. Clip the corners and turn the material right-side-out, pulling the corners out with a pin to make them neat. Lightly press the edges with an iron if you like, but keep in mind that unironed, plump seams can add a luxurious finish.

STEP 3. Hand-sew down the center of the rectangle of tulle and satin with gathering stitches; pull and knot the threads. Wrap the 2-yard piece of ribbon around the gathered center of the bow and tie it in a knot.

STEP 4. Hand-sew the three fabric roses to the center of the bow. Tie ⅓ of a yard of tulle in a casual bow and hand-sew it to the back of the satin bow. Add ribbon streamers under the roses if you desire. Finish by sewing the cording or the 18-inch length of ribbon to the back of the bow for a tie.

Beaded Silk Bows

This silk embroidered taffeta bow has gorgeous sheen and the pearl beads make lovely white-on-white accents. Use it to decorate aisles and pews, or gather table skirts into elegant swags and pin a bow to the center of each.

COST: *Approximately $20* TIME: *4–6 hours* LEVEL: *3* DO: *4–6 months before the wedding, especially if you will need several*

YOU WILL NEED (FOR ONE BOW):

- Scissors
- Tape measure
- Piece of 10- by 36-inch silk embroidered fabric with all-over repeat embroidered design
- Piece of 9- by 18-inch low-loft quilt batting
- Sewing machine
- Sewing needle and sewing thread to match fabric

- Beading thread
- 30 gram package of 3mm pearls
- Beaded trim, 4 inches long, 1-inch wide
- 3–4 yards of 108-inch-wide tulle (optional)

STEP 1. Cut a 10- by 36-inch length of the silk fabric. Cut one 9- by 18-inch piece of low-loft quilt batting, and set it aside. Fold the piece of silk fabric in half so that you have a 10- by 18-inch rectangle. Sew three sides, leaving one end open. Turn the fabric right-side-out, and press the edges flat with your fingertips, pulling the corners out with a pin so that they're neat. You will now have what looks like a small pillowcase. Insert the piece of batting into the sewn piece of silk, making sure that the corners are filled. Tuck the open end in ½ inch and pin it closed. Stitch the closed end with a sewing machine or by hand, and remove the pins.

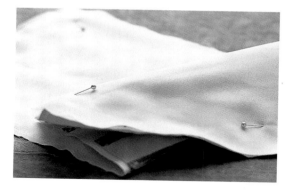

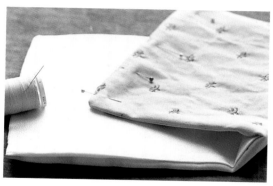

STEP 2. Fill a dish with beads so they will be easy to pick up. (Unless your beads are

Wrap approximately 3 yards by 108 inches of tulle around the back of a chair. You might need to play with the draping of the material until you are satisfied with the way it looks. Gather the loose ends of the tulle with a ribbon to hold them place. Pin the beaded bow to the center of the back of the chair.

packaged on a strand, in which case it is easier to pull one off at a time.) With the beading thread and needle, sew the pearls onto the embroidered patterns in the fabric. Let the patterns guide you. You can just use one bead in the center of each design, or sew a cluster. You can decide how many you want. Hide the knots and running threads inside the batting if you don't want them to show on the back of the bow.

STEP 3. Gather the bow in the center with your hand, wrap the piece of beaded trim around the center and stitch it to the fabric.

Flower Girl's Basket

The flower girl's entrance is one of the most precious moments of the ceremony. Giving her this adorable hand-decorated basket to carry her rose petals in will make her feel important and special. The basket itself is covered completely with silk roses, and the handle is wrapped in ribbon. Using the same technique, you could decorate a similar basket with fresh flowers. Both would be perfect for the flower girl to use for her walk down the aisle.

❧COST: *Approximately $35–$60*   ❧TIME: *Less than 1 hour*   ❧LEVEL: *1*   ❧DO: *Do the night before or the morning of the wedding day if you are using fresh flowers. Do anytime before the wedding if you are using silk flowers.*

YOU WILL NEED

- ❧ *15-inch-wide basket with handle*
- ❧ *Silk or fresh flowers (approximately two dozen 4-inch blooms for a 15-inch-wide basket)*

- ❧ *Wire clippers*
- ❧ *Scissors*
- ❧ *Glue gun*
- ❧ *1 ½ yards of 1-inch-wide ribbon*

STEP 1. Remove all stems and leaves from the silk flowers. If you're using fresh flowers, cut the stems to 1 inch and soak them in a sink or pan of water, preferably overnight.

STEP 2. Using a glue gun, attach the flowers to the basket, starting at the bottom. Go all around the basket, and then repeat, going around again and again until you have covered the entire basket with blooms. Wrap the ribbon around and around the handle, covering it completely and tying it with thread where the handle meets the basket so the ribbon doesn't unravel. Tie two ribbon bows and glue one on each end of the handle. If you are using fresh flowers, lightly mist them with water and store the basket in a plastic bag in a cool place until you are ready to use it. You can also mist the flowers just before setting the basket out.

REUSE THE BASKET

At the reception, a container for holding cards at the gift table is essential. Many guests send gifts or cards by mail before the wedding; however, some prefer to bring a card with a check enclosed on the wedding day. This flowered basket is perfect for keeping all the cards and good wishes in one place.

Beaded Silk Ringbearer's Pillow

Besides "You may now kiss the bride," the words "With this ring, I thee wed" are the most climactic in a traditional wedding ceremony. If you elect to have a ringbearer come down the aisle and make a formal presentation, a beautiful handmade ring pillow adds to an already dramatic procession. Make this beaded, embroidered silk ring pillow accented with a circle of roses around its edge. The beadwork is easy—just follow the outline of the embroidery in the fabric with tiny pearl and crystal beads. Buy the best silk satin or silk taffeta you can afford. The fabric might be expensive, but you'll only need a small piece.

COST: *Approximately $30*   TIME: *About a weekend*   LEVEL: *3 (level 2 without beadwork)*   DO: *3–4 months before the wedding*

- ❧ *Satin or taffeta embroidered fabric (½ yard)*
- ❧ *Two 18- by 18-inch squares of low-loft quilt batting*
- ❧ *Two 18- by 18-inch squares of muslin*
- ❧ *Straight pins*
- ❧ *Sewing machine*
- ❧ *Sewing needle and thread to match fabric**
- ❧ *1 small bag poly stuffing*
- ❧ *12-inch embroidery hoop*
- ❧ *1 strand of 3mm pearl beads (or one 3mm package)*
- ❧ *1 dozen 3mm Austrian crystal beads*
- ❧ *Beading thread*
- ❧ *Pencil*
- ❧ *Scissors*
- ❧ *Tape measure*
- ❧ *One 18- by 18-inch square of paper*
- ❧ *30 inches of braid edging*
- ❧ *3 ½ dozen premade ½-inch rosettes*

*I prefer to use a sewing needle for beading. I test it first to see if it fits through the hole in my beads. A beading needle can be difficult for a beginner to thread.

STEP 1. Cut two 18- by 18-inch squares of embroidered satin, two 18- by 18-inch squares of quilt batting (the quilt batting prevents your pillow from looking lumpy when you stuff it with poly-fill), and two 18- by 18-inch squares of muslin fabric. Layer one square of satin fabric over one square of quilt batting and one square of muslin. Pin and then baste all the layers together to hold. Repeat the process with another three layers of fabric (this will be the backing for the pillow) and set them aside. Take the first layered fabric "sandwich" and put it into the embroidery hoop. Stretch the fabric across it so it's taut and tighten the hoop.

STEP 2. Thread the needle with an 18-inch length of beading thread, and knot the end. Coming from underneath the hoop, insert the needle so it comes out precisely on one of the vines or flowers upon which you want to stitch a bead. Pull the thread all the way through, letting the knot catch, and then slip a bead over the needle and push it down

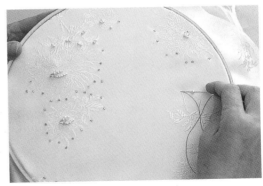

to the fabric. Insert the needle as close to the bead as you can and pull it through to the side underneath. Repeat this step for all the beads. You can judge how much beading you want on your pillow. The underneath threads will be visible, but take care not to drag the under-threads too much because they might pucker the fabric.

STEP 3. When you have completed your beadwork, remove the fabric sandwich from the hoop. Put the embroidery hoop on top of the piece of construction paper; measure and draw a circle 1 inch wider all around than the hoop, and cut out the circle you've drawn. Make small notches around the edge of the paper circle at 2-inch intervals (see photo below).

STEP 4. Using the paper pattern you have just made, cut a circle from the beaded fabric as well as from the layers of backing fabric (see photo, top right). With the right sides

facing, pin the beaded circle and the backing fabric and hand-stitch around the edge of the circle with basting stitches to hold. Using the pattern as a guide, cut notches in the fabric (see photo, bottom right). Sew around the circle, leaving a ½-inch seam allowance and a 3-inch opening for turning the pillow.

STEP 5. Turn the circle right-side-out, shaping the pillow at the same time by pressing the edges with your fingers. Stuff the pillow with poly-fill and continue to mold it into a round shape. When you are satisfied with the roundness, close the opening with tiny hand stitches. Hand-stitch the braid around the seam edge of the pillow (see photo, top left). The cording also provides a nice shelf for the rosettes.

STEP 6. Hand-stitch or hot-glue the rosettes to the top of the braid (see photo below). Tie two 24-inch lengths of ribbon together with a knot. Stitch the knot to the center of the pillow. (The ribbon ends are for tying the wedding rings to the pillow.)

Antique Lace
Ringbearer's Pillow

*T*his is an excellent opportunity for using a scrap of your grandmother's wedding gown or some heirloom lace. You could also use a scrap of new lace from your own wedding gown if you are having it custom-made.

COST: About $2 to $10   TIME: 1 hour or less   LEVEL: 1   DO: At least 2 months before the wedding

YOU WILL NEED

- *Two 5-inch-square pieces of fabric, preferable ivory or white*
- *Pieces of lace to cover top of pillow*
- *Ribbon*
- *Sewing needle and thread*
- *Beading thread*
- *Small bag of poly stuffing*
- *Sewing machine*
- *Fabric marking pencil*
- *Rosettes*

Optional items for other trims:
- *Beads*
- *Trims*
- *Cording*
- *Old jewelry*
- *Tassels*

STEP 1. Cut two 5-inch squares of fabric. Stitch around all the sides with a ½-inch seam allowance, and leave a 3-inch opening on one end. Trim the corners to remove bulk, and turn the fabric right-side-out. Press the edges lightly with an iron if you like, and pull out the corner ends with a pin. Stuff the opening with enough poly-fill to make the pillow plump, then stitch the opening closed with tiny overlapping stitches.

STEP 2. Trim the pillow with rosettes, ribbon ties, beads, or tassels—let your imagination be your guide. Finish by sewing streamers of ribbon to the center of the pillow to secure the rings.

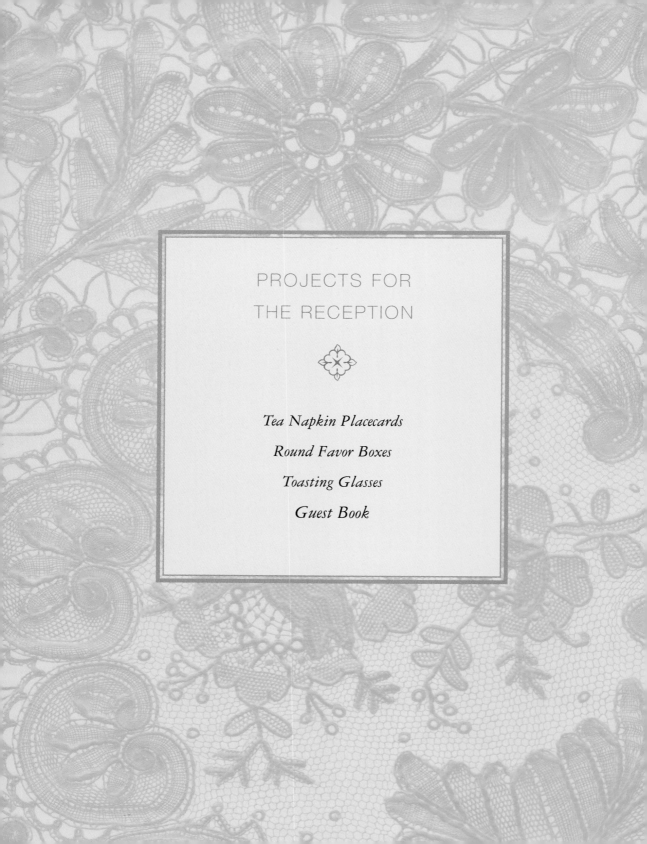

PROJECTS FOR
THE RECEPTION

Tea Napkin Placecards

Round Favor Boxes

Toasting Glasses

Guest Book

Tea Napkin Placecards

The ceremony is over, your guests have gathered at the reception site, and everyone is ready to sit down and enjoy a nice meal. Placecards will guarantee that all the guests know where to sit and will also make them feel recognized! Don't go to a lot of trouble—just attach each placecard to a crisp white tea napkin with a pretty ribbon and some fresh lavender or dried violets.

✤COST: *$1.00–$2.50 per napkin* ✤TIME: *Minutes* ✤LEVEL: *1* ✤DO: *At least 1 month before the wedding*

YOU WILL NEED

- Tea napkins
- Organza ribbon (one 12-inch long, ½-inch wide piece per napkin)
- Name cards
- Fresh flowers (such as lavender) or dried flowers

Round Favor Boxes

iving each wedding guest a small gift or favor has become a popular tradition. Whether the ceremony is traditional or contemporary, a favor such as the round boxes featured here is a simple yet eloquent expression of a couple's appreciation for their guests' participation in their big day. Fill your completed boxes with bags containing candy, flower seeds, or something else that represents the particular style of your wedding. The technique for making these favors can be adapted to create all kinds of other little boxes using small artificial flowers and different lace or fabric trims. Ask your family and friends to help make these boxes. It will be a good opportunity to relax, enjoy each other's company, and discuss the details of the upcoming event.

✿COST: *$2–$3 per box* ✿ TIME: *Less than 1 hour* ✿LEVEL: *1* ✿DO: *3–4 months before the wedding*

- Cardboard dowel from paper towel roll
- Craft knife
- Pencil
- Scissors
- Construction paper
- 2-inch square of tissue paper for each box
- Glue gun
- Small craft brush (for glue)
- One package (36) craft leaves (you'll need about 12 leaves for one box)
- Small plastic bags for the candy or seeds
- Candy or flower seeds
- 3 premade silk roses 2 ½ by 2 ½ inches wide or handmade fabric roses (see instructions on page 46)
- Ribbon

STEP 1. Cut the cardboard dowel into 3-inch sections with a craft knife. Using the pencil, trace the base of a piece of the dowel onto a piece of construction paper; this will become the favor box bottom. Draw another circle ½ inch outside the circumference of the first penciled circle; cut out the bigger circle with scissors. Cut tabs all around the circle, stopping at the penciled line. The box bottom should now look like the base to a paper cup with edges that fold up. Place the circle at the bottom of the dowel, fold the edges up, dot the insides of the tabs with glue, and glue them to the sides of the dowel.

STEP 2. Using the glue gun and the craft brush to spread the glue evenly, attach leaves to the top of the dowel, extending the points up over the top ½ inch of the box with the glue gun. Continue overlapping and gluing until the box is completely covered. Fill the box with candy or seeds that have been placed in small plastic bags. Tuck the silk or fabric rose inside the top of the box where the leaves extend; the rose is the box lid. Wrap a length of ribbon around the box and tie it in a bow.

Patterned China Centerpieces

lowers are among the most eye-catching and important wedding decorations. They can express the season and color scheme of your wedding, and they make a room come alive. The containers in which you arrange the flowers can be almost as eye-catching. Explore your cupboard and pantry, looking for silver, china, crystal bowls, and baskets. Fine patterned china tureens make elegant, graceful centerpieces: they can also have sentimental value if the china has been passed down through generations in your family. Remember that the arrangement doesn't have to be perfect. The flowers themselves are beautiful, and your guests are not going to be looking for imperfections. *Note:* Line the container with a plastic bag to protect it from possible water damage.

❧COST: *Approximately $35* ❧TIME: *1 hour* ❧LEVEL: *1* ❧DO: *Make this arrangement the day before or the morning of the wedding. Keep it in a cool place until the reception.*

YOU WILL NEED
(FOR ONE CENTERPIECE):

- Approximately 1 ½ dozen roses or a dozen roses and about 6 other flowers and greenery for filler
- Scissors or pruning shears
- Water
- Decorative container such as a china soup tureen or bowl
- Kitchen knife
- Block of wet floral foam—cut to fit container
- Plastic bag to fit container
- Roll of Grip 'n Stick adhesive floral tape
- Water mister

STEP 1. Assemble all the supplies. Fill your sink or a large container with water. You might want to use newspaper to protect surfaces and collect discarded foliage. Trim all the leaves from the stems and any wilted petals from the roses and other flowers; cut the stems underwater with a clipper or scissors and leave them in water in a refrigerated place until you are ready to arrange them.

STEP 2. Cut the floral foam with a knife or scissors if necessary to fit the container you will be using. (See photo next page.) A tight fit is best. Soak the floral foam in water for two minutes. You will know if the floral foam is soaked completely because it will be quite heavy. You will need to line the container with a plastic bag. Press three lengths of the Grip 'n Stick adhesive tape to the bot-

STEP 3. Put the wet floral foam into the container. Begin trimming and inserting flowers that have been cut to the height you desire into the floral foam at the center of the container, working your way from the center outward. We used rose sprays for this arrangement because they have more blooms per stem. You can also use branches and other flowers for filler. Stand back and take a look at your arrangement to make sure it has a pleasing shape and to see if any area needs more flowers. A centerpiece looks best if all sides are filled in with flowers. Mist the bouquet with water just before you set it out. Always keep flowers in a cool area.

tom of the container, and press the bag into the sticky tape to hold it in place. *Be certain you have purchased floral foam that is fresh and designed to be used wet. If the foam does not absorb the water, your flowers will probably wilt.*

PLEIN AIR CENTER- PIECES

For a casual, outdoor reception, flowers can be arranged in pretty baskets, metal buckets, or even household paint cans that have been wrapped with pretty ribbons.

Toasting Glasses

fter the cake is cut and before the dancing begins, it's customary for the guests to raise their glasses in a toast to the bride and groom. Make them feel like a king and queen by decorating a pair of lovely crystal champagne glasses with crystal and silver beads. Then no detail will have been overlooked! The bubbles and the beads will catch the light and make the glasses sparkle. You can use antique glasses, and even if they are not a perfect match, their fluid shapes will make a complementary pair, just as do the bride and groom. Embellish the stems of the glasses with a whimsical beaded wire attached to beaded satin bows.

COST: *About $5* TIME: *About 2 hours* LEVEL: *2* DO: *At least 1 month before the wedding*

- ❧ *2 champagne glasses*
- ❧ *One 30 gram package of crystal beads*
- ❧ *One 30 gram tube or package of 3mm silver beads (Rocailles)*
- ❧ *Beading wire (36 inches)*
- ❧ *Satin ribbon (½ yard long, 1 inch wide)*
- ❧ *Tacky white craft glue*
- ❧ *Dish for beads*
- ❧ *Thread and needle*
- ❧ *Pencil*
- ❧ *Needle-nose pliers*

STEP 1. Cut four 3-inch lengths of ribbon. Put your finger in the center, fold each top edge down and smooth it so that you have a small triangle. Pin the center edges. With a needle and thread, sew running stitches across the bottom of the folded ribbon—pull the thread to gather the fabric, and tack it to hold. The piece of ribbon should now look like a leaf. Knot the thread and put the "leaf" aside. Repeat this step with the other three pieces of ribbon.

STEP 2. Pour the silver Rocaille beads into a small dish. Squeeze glue on two of the ribbon leaves, and press them glue-side-down into the dish of beads. Set them aside and let them dry for about ten minutes.

STEP 3. Sew one beaded leaf and one plain leaf together at their raw, gathered edges.

Sew a rhinestone button over the seam where the two leaves are joined (see photo, top right). Repeat this step for the other two leaves.

STEP 4. Cut two lengths of beading wire 21 inches long. Wrap the wire around a pencil to give it a spiral shape. Thread one bead on the end of the wire and wrap a small amount of wire around the bead with the needle-nose pliers to secure the end. Continue to thread crystal beads onto the wire until the loops of the spiral are full of beads. It's okay to have some gaps between the beads. Wrap the other end of the beaded wire around the last bead on the spiral with the pliers to lock the end. Wrap one end of the finished piece of beaded wire around the button of the silk bow (see bottom photo), and twist the rest of the beaded wire around the stem of the champagne glass.

Note: You should be able to easily remove the decoration to wash the glasses.

Guest Book

You can make this guest book in minutes with a large hardcover sketchbook or a photo album with archival paper (rather than one with adhesive pages), a glue gun, and some pretty designer paper. Decorate the cover even more by gluing a silk ribbon corsage in the left hand corner with some antique buttons.

COST: Approximately $10 ❧ *TIME: ½ hour* ❧ *LEVEL: 1* ❧ *DO: Anytime before the wedding day*

YOU WILL NEED:

- *1 sheet of designer paper large enough to fit the cover of your guest book*
- *Scissors*
- *Hot-glue gun*
- *Trims*
- *Beads*
- *Buttons*
- *Pieces of ribbon*
- *Rosettes*

Measure the dimensions of your book, and then cut a piece of designer paper to fit the inside borders of the book's cover. Glue the the paper to the front cover of the book, smoothing it carefully so there are no wrinkles or bumps. Using the glue gun, adhere the trims around the paper to make an outer border, and then glue buttons, ribbon bows, beads, or rosettes to the corners of the paper. You can use whatever you think will look pretty. Set the book out on the cake table or the gift table at the reception for your guests to sign.

CHAPTER 7

Happily Ever After

"And they lived happily ever after" are usually the last words of a fairy tale. In real life, a wedding marks the beginning of a story. You'll have loads of people to thank for their gifts and lots of pictures to develop and sort through. Your wedding pictures capture the different high points and features of the occasion—the bride and groom, your guests, the cake, and the flowers. Save your favorites in an album or photo box so that you can revisit your wedding day and share your memories with family and friends. Make picture frames in which to put special photographs and either give them as gifts or keep them for yourself.

Rose Covered Memory Box

A wedding memory box is a lovely alternative to the traditional "wedding album." Decorate an art portfolio box with fabric, ribbon, trims, and fabric roses. Wedding portraits can be matted or bonded to mat board and tied with a satin ribbon bow before being tucked into the box. The ribbon tie makes the portraits easy to lift out of the box. Have your local frame shop cut the mats to size. You might also have the professional framer bond the photos to the mat board or frame them with mat board. You could also use this box to store videos or snapshots of the wedding. You can find boxes at stationery, artist supply, and paper stores.

❧COST: *About $20*   ❧TIME: *A good weekend project*   ❧LEVEL: *2*   ❧DO: *Anytime before or after the wedding*

YOU WILL NEED:

- *1 acid-free box, approximately 11 by 14 inches*
- *Fabric to cover top of box (½ yard)*
- *11- by 14-inch piece of low-loft quilt batting*
- *Tacky glue or glue gun*
- *Photographic dry spray-mount*
- *Straight pins*
- *3 yards of braided trim*
- *2 yards of 2-inch-wide ribbon to tie around the box*

- *Twenty 2-inch-diameter fabric roses (see p. 46) or other silk flowers*
- *Needle and thread*
- *Purchase these items from a professional frame shop:*
- *Acid-free mat board in black or desired color trimmed to fit inside box—one dozen*
- *12 sheets acid-free tissue paper*

STEP 1. Cut a piece of fabric to fit the top and the sides of the box lid. The fabric will need to come only to the lower/bottom edge of the lid's sides because you will cover the raw edge of fabric with decorative trim. Cut a rectangle of quilt batting to the exact size of the box top (11 by 14 inches).

STEP 2. Attach the quilt batting to the top of the box lid with tacky glue or dry mount-spray and let it dry. (Do not extend the bat-

ting over the sides of the lid.) Center the fabric on the batting and pin it securely. Fold the fabric at the corners just as you

would wrap a package, cutting away any excess fabric for a nice, neat corner. Use a glue gun to adhere the fabric to the lid's sides.

STEP 3. With a glue gun, attach the braided trims around the lid sides to cover the raw edges of the fabric and to give them a nice tailored finish (see photo, bottom left). Fold a 1½ yard length of ribbon in half. Wrap the ribbon around the center of the box so that you have extra ribbon extending for the decorative tie. Tack the ribbon to the lid using the glue gun. (The roses will cover the glued ribbon.) Attach the roses to the lid of the box with the glue gun.

STEP 4. Have a professional frame shop cut twelve acid-free mat boards and twelve acid-free tissue sheets to fit inside the box. (The box has room for about twelve.) Also have the professional framer attach the photographs to the mat board. Tie the matted photos in a bundle with a pretty ribbon and store them inside the box.

Beaded Picture Frame

*A*ll you will need to make this sparkling frame is glue, crystal beads, and scraps of rhinestone jewelry. A special multi-purpose cement glue (BOND-527) available at craft stores makes gluing beads to glass easy. It dries to a nice clear finish and you can scrape off any accidental drips on your frame with a razor blade after you have finished your project.

COST: *About $15* TIME: *About 1/2 hour* LEVEL: *1* DO: *Anytime before or after the wedding*

YOU WILL NEED:

- Cardboard or newspaper for work surface
- 1 plain glass frame
- BOND-527 glue
- Tweezers
- Dish for beads
- 1 package 3mm crystal beads
- Pieces of rhinestone jewelry
- Damp cloth for clean-up

STEP 1. The first thing to do is set out all of your supplies and prepare your work space. Pour the beads into a dish, and lay out a piece of cardboard or newspaper to cover and protect your work surface. Open a window or work in a well ventilated area because the glue has strong fumes. Lay out the pieces of jewelry in the order in which you plan to attach them to your frame.

STEP 2. Squeeze a thin line of glue on the frame in the shape in which you want to arrange the crystal beads. The glue dries slowly enough so that you have time to pick up the beads with your tweezers and set them in the glue. Let the beads set and the glue dry (this should take about five minutes or so, depending on the humidity in your area). Apply more glue to the parts of the frame where you want your pieces of rhinestone. Again, use the tweezers to firmly press the jewels into the glue.

STEP 3. When you have finished decorating your frame, let the project dry thoroughly overnight. Use a razor blade to scrape off any accidental drops of glue. Your frame is now ready to use—select a particularly nice photograph from the wedding and put it on your dresser or mantle as a keepsake.

Thank-You Notes

These thank-you notes, like the engagement and bridal shower invitations, are one of a kind. As you have done for several of the projects in this book, make them with pieces of antique or new lace, decorative paper, silk flowers, and cardstock. You can of course use other elements such as photographs, pressed flowers, or beads. This is your opportunity to make your guests feel as special and appreciated as they made you feel—go the extra mile and give them a personal, handmade thank-you.

COST: *About $2 per card*   TIME: *30 minutes*   LEVEL: *1*   DO: *About 4 weeks after the wedding*

YOU WILL NEED:

- *Plain cards and envelopes*
- *Scraps of ribbon and lace*
- *Dried or pressed flowers*
- *Scraps of decorative paper*
- *2–3 yards of ¼-inch-wide ribbon*

- *Double sided scotch tape*
- *One sided scotch tape*
- *Craft glue*
- *Paper cutter*
- *Scissors*

STEP 1. Cut a square of card stock to fit in the size envelope you have chosen, unless you bought envelopes with their own blank cards. Cut a smaller square of decorative paper and attach it to the center top, middle, or bottom of the card with double sided scotch tape.

STEP 2. Cut a length of lace, pretty ribbon, or other decorative fabric and attach it to the center of the decorative paper with double-sided scotch tape. Tie a ribbon around the side of the card near the fold. Hold the bow in place with double-sided tape or glue. Write a personal message inside.

Index